STANDING

on

Top of the Mountain

DAWN HAMILTON

AuthorHouse™
1663 Liberty Drive
Bloomington, IN 47403
www.authorhouse.com
Phone: 1 (800) 839-8640

Published by AuthorHouse 06/18/2015

ISBN: 978-1-5049-1620-2 (sc)
ISBN: 978-1-5049-1621-9 (e)

Library of Congress Control Number: 2015909249

Print information available on the last page.

Any people depicted in stock imagery provided by Thinkstock are models, and such images are being used for illustrative purposes only. Certain stock imagery © Thinkstock.

This book is printed on acid-free paper.

Because of the dynamic nature of the Internet, any web addresses or links contained in this book may have changed since publication and may no longer be valid. The views expressed in this work are solely those of the author and do not necessarily reflect the views of the publisher, and the publisher hereby disclaims any responsibility for them.

CONTENTS

To my parents,Frederick and Rebecca McCaulsky Hamilton
Uncle Lloyd and aunt Bev
My grandparents, Bernard and Jestina McCaulsky
Papa and mum

Mercella Edwards (Miss Dolly),

my children, Graceann and Horace Long,
#Shadesbygal#and Junior

for all that I am. Thank you with all my love

INTRODUCTION

I was not a teenager who expressed my feelings, so while I was attending an all-ages school in Jamaica, West Indies, I found myself writing down the pain I was feeling in a journal my mom had given me. It became my freedom. I did not realize then that it would become my horizon along life's pathway. Writing sustains me through difficult times. It is the only way I know how to deal with hardships both emotionally and physically. I call the journal entries "my letters to God," praying that when he responds, I will hear his voice.

To endure is difficult, but to deal with physical and verbal abuse is heartrending. I thank God every day for giving me a voice through my writing and making a difference to someone along the way. My main reason for writing this book it is to help young girls and women who are going through or have been through physical, verbal, and emotional abuse, rape, homelessness, and joblessness. You are not alone, and there is always hope.

I want to let you know that with faith and strong persistence, you won't lose your self-esteem, but instead you will build confidence within yourself. You do not have to stay in any situation for any reason whatsoever, for we are all overcomers. Yes, I've been angry, and I've felt rage; however, I turned these emotions into positive forces.

I have built my life on the philosophy that my corner of the world will not be the same just because I have passed this way. So in my journey I have decided to touch as many lives as possible, and I believe the circulation of this book will allow me to touch even more lives. I would like to remind others to believe in themselves, their goals, and their dreams because they will become what they believe.

TO MY SON, HORACE (JUNIOR)

It was a rainy night when a son was born—with so many complications—

But it was my dedication to God that kept him in syndication.

There were doctors and nurses everywhere.

What they didn't know was my God was near when Horace was not doing well.

But in Jesus' hands he dwelt; I was there with him hours on end.

But it was my voice he heard in the end.

It was not an easy task for him through the years, but

He believes in me, and

I believe in God,

The one that made everything under the sun,

And I thank Him for being the guiding force for our son.

For all the love that I ever gave, it falls right back on you, and for that, I thank God.

To My Daughter (Amazing Grace)

My dream started with you.

Having you changed my whole life.

If it wasn't for you, I know I would be living a completely different way.

But God knew best—you were loved before I even knew you.

I wanted you to become so much.

It gives me the drive to strive.

Destiny has its own way—I thought it was a dream, but in the end, my destiny was found in you.

—From Mom, with all my love.

SHAWNA KAY

You are special.
You are love.
You can be whatever you want to be.
You are young and radiant.
I know you will grow gracefully.
Believe in yourself—that you can—
And with storm clouds, hold on.
Life comes with twists, turns and road blocks
See me in your dreams
One day I will be back

HOW YOU TREAT OTHERS

Never forget the road you travel.

Treat others the way you would like to be treated.

It took hard work to get you where you are today,

But it takes only a moment to take you back to where you were.

So before you forget where you came from,

Remember the journey that took you there.

THE INDEPENDENT WOMAN

Anchors her life on what she wants.
She is driven—passionate—very ambitious.
The independent woman knows what is her
Difference and makes it.
She practices what she preaches.
Her character speaks for itself.
The independent woman hurts,
Eventually takes it, has a lesson learned,
And keeps it moving.
She is vulnerable but holds on to her power.
The independent woman knows who she is.
She diligently embraces the beauty that
Surrounds her.
She can be her worst enemy or find her
Greatest strength within herself.
The independent woman—
Is she you? She can be.
I am sure she is me.

IMAGINE

Imagine yourself living in a shack—
No book bag to carry on your back,
Holes in your shoes,
And having to go to school.
Imagine looking into a mirror,
Your mind racing:
My dad the caretaker, died
Leaving mommy a widow
Do I dare dream?
I fell down on my knees.
God, I know You see my needs.
"My dear, I have always been here.
I have been waiting."
I felt the wind brush by my ear.

BEING ME

I am something else.
I know.
I am determined.
That's my faith.
Independent,
Very outspoken—
It's one of my flaws.
I make mistakes, not excuses.
At times I lose control.

I am a work in progress at all times.
I used to be a sucker for sad stories—
Not anymore.
Seventy percent of them are not true.
I used to carry a lot of overweight baggage.
I shed it along my journey.
I have grown through my scars and
Become the best at just being me.

YOUR TOUCH

You have touched my life—
So much so,
I want to strive.
You have touched my life
Like no other.
Compared to you
Could only be my mother.
You have touched my life,
Wiped away my tears,
And brought back my smile.
You have touched my life
In more ways than one.
Sometimes I don't even know
How to respond.
You have touched my life
So dearly.

Now I can see more clearly.
You have touched my life
So deeply.
You have changed my perception
completely.
You touched my life
When I was down
And gave me confidence
I had never known.
You have touched my heart
And mended
What was once torn apart.
You have touched my life!
And replaced complexity
With honest simplicity
You continue to touch my life

When I am miles away and alone
Because you constantly burn up
the phone
Your touch is sweet
Sometimes I don't need to eat
Honey now that you have touched
me with your blessings
Promise me it will never end
because you have touch my life
And me made me whole again

8

Believe in You

If you can be still at times and see what a remarkably different your life can be with faith, It will give you complete trust and confidence in God and yourself.

If you cannot be loyal to yourself, have confidence within yourself, trust yourself, and stay real.

Everything starts with you. Once you acknowledge that control and power start from within, your faith and belief will become one, for you will know then that you do not have to see the success in front of you to believe you can achieve success.

You already know from within that you can achieve, accomplish, stay real, and make a difference because your faith has brought forth your hope and belief.

Once you acknowledge how powerful and influential you can be in your own life you will have the power to uphold your purpose and be the difference. It is because of your faith in believing that you receive.

YOU WILL NEVER KNOW

Never be afraid to challenge yourself.
You will never know until you try.

Never be afraid to be yourself.
This is the best way to be.

Never be afraid to act, because you may be just
The person who makes the difference.

And never be afraid to count on people,
Because they may be the ones who count on you.

WHO IS CONCERN?

Jealousy stirs up animosity,
So love is concern.
Do not let anyone tell you who you should be; you are your own person, so it is up to you.
Know who you are "If you don't"your heart is concern.

When you live to please, you will never be at ease with yourself,
So God is concern.

When trouble comes your way, you want to reach out to someone for a helping hand, and when there is no one to show you compassion, you should be concerned.

Rejection and persecution we all bear, but they are only a test for you to pass, for burdens do not last.

Victory you can win, if only you remain strong.
You do not need to prove to anyone how richly you are blessed.

Take inventory, re-assess yourself, and give life your "ultimate effort".

GOD WILL DO IT FOR YOU

Don't you know there is nothing that God wouldn't
do for you?
He did it for Elisha and Jeremiah;
He will do it for you.
He did it for Samuel and Daniel;
He will do it for you.
He did it for Joshua and Jonah;
He will do it for you.

He did it for Abraham and Simon;
He will do it for you.
He has done it for me;
He will do it for you.
His list goes on and on.
If you want to be true to yourself,
You will know He is the only one you can truly
depend on.

"Living"

Do not be with someone because you are desperate for material gain.
Your living will surely be in vain.
No one should enter a relationship for vanity.
It should be for love, happiness, and prosperity.

"INDULGE"

Take time out from the hustle and bustle of your daily life, and exhale. Spend some quality time with yourself. Know who you are, and believe in what you do. Nurture your life. Pamper yourself and examine your being. Life can be such a luxury.
It has no limitation on prosperity.

"Because of Fear"

Do not let anyone come into your life to take charge of it. Do not allow yourself to be threatened and beaten
on top of it. Do not stand for it, for what you see in the beginning is how it will end.
Do not let people tell you they cannot make it without you,
For what will be done to you, you cannot take it. And in the end it will not worth it.

"Just Life"

Life will not always go the way you desire.

Accept that you have experienced a bad encounter, and recover.

Not everything that glitters is gold, and a lot of us fail to realize that what you see sometimes is not what you get.

But because of human desires, we allow ourselves to be taken into situations that are not worthy of our qualities. Tell yourself you are worth far more than you are receiving; if someone doesn't want your apples, don't let that person shake your tree.

CONFIDENCE

To gain confidence within ourselves
Take a look in the mirror tell yourself,
"Enough feeling sorry for myself."
Say, "I can. I know I can,
I believe I can."
Move yourself out of situations that
are not worth your time.
Living does not have a time limit.
But time is limited
Sometimes we create our own problems
Because we are used to them
Forget *used to* and get *wise to*.

Sickness

Sickness shows no discrimination.

It can devour anyone at any time regardless of how noble we are

 So be conscious of

The way you live because your health can

Erupt when you least expect it.

We are never too rich to fall downward and

Never too large to be conquered.

You did not bring yourself into the world.

Therefore, you are not your own.

Learn to be humble, and when you reach the

Upward heights of progressiveness and are

Stricken by an illness, you will not be alone.

MIX UP

We need to stop talking where there is too much gossiping,
For we certainly will have some betraying and condemning
It is not healthy living
We do not always know others circumstances
That is why we have to keep on praying
There are times we have to go on fasting
So that God can perform His healing
Life is not about backbiting or pretending
It is about forgiving and loving
Stop all the hating, for it profit us nothing

I Survived

I survived because I wanted to prove that my experiences are not what I am, but as I journeyed through the dark alleys. I realized I could not be a people pleaser and survive, for that weight alone was a heavy burden to carry with the occurrences I had been enduring.

It was a self-destructive hazard down there, but a voice within me said, "If you can go through all this to prove who you are to someone else, why not release yourself from proving and restore your joy by being yourself." I listened to the voice and let go.

I let go of the prison I locked myself into, weaken by fear, rejections, adversities, depression, low self-esteem, and anger, and I started to trust myself to believe that I could and would rise above. I continued the journey because through my determination, I have gained enough strength to see a glimmer of light from the distant I was at the end of the alley.

With my personal growth and self-healing I know that I am a survivor and can make a difference, for I have survived.

PERSISTENCE

No one should say, "I accept whatever comes my way"

The way you choose to go through life is your decision

The essence of change is always in your hands

If you feel you are being suffocated by a situation, make a change

You will get only what you seek

If you have the capability to sustain every potential you seek

And aim higher than you believe you can reach,

Then by your own belief, you can achieve any goal

If you are willing to be persistent

PRAYER CAN

Prayer is the most powerful source there is. It can move any stumbling block or barrier

Prayer works miracles

Look around you and see someone is praying

Prayer changes things

It even reverses intention

Prayer is a miracle-working remedy but has to be sincere

It is the one and only resource that makes the remarkable difference in all things

You just have to take the moment to notice

God answers prayers

Take the moment to listen

Sometimes it is not the answer we want, so we ignore his reply

We may not see the manifestation of His answer at the present time,

But eventually it reveals itself to us

BE THE DIFFERENCE

Others will take your good intentions and tell you it seems like you are looking for attention.

If God wants you to be the difference to certain situations,

Never mind the convictions.

He finds favor in you to be an inspiration.

Do not live your life in someone's reflection.

God's expectation of you is to let His people know they can have salvation.

FRIENDSHIP

Friendship should not be taken for granted.
There are times when we need to be lifted up,
Times when we need to be encouraged,
Times when we need a helping hand,
Times when we need a listening ear
You can be that type of friend to someone
It is a friendship that comes with truth and sincerity
It values more than diamonds, pearls, and gold
It cannot be bought or sold.
The beautiful thing about friendship
It will be there with us as we grow old.

YOUR WILDEST DREAM

Why live in uncertainty when there is potential?

Understand that circumstances may hold you back temporarily, but believe in yourself.

It may seem like your dreams crumble inside of you, but they don't.

They are just hidden beneath the clouds, and as the clouds devolve, the rainbow you see is the opportunity to let the sunshine through.

Usher in the magnificent hour to see the spectacular view, and it could be beyond your wildest dreams.

"It takes Courage"

Do not allow anyone to take away your will power, self-esteem, self-image, self-worth, or faith in yourself. Hurtful words, criticism, and put-downs can be traumatic to the depths of your soul. They weaken your inner strength. You want to move forward, but those hurtful words haunt you like the invisible ghost that they are. When a person who does not have anything nice to say or support the good you are doing wants to hold you back from progress, this is selfishness, which is very common these days.

The worst thing to do is to live in someone else's shadows. Do your thing and make your difference.

Opportunity comes by chance and sometimes once.

You have the beauty and the will, and you are rare.

God never made any one of us exactly alike. That is why you are unique.

Express what you got, even when others keep putting you down.

It is only because they know you got it.

You cannot go back and change your yesterday, but you certainly can produce your difference today.

TO YOURSELF BE FAITHFUL

Bring forth your passion by doing what you like to do.

Live your life to the fullest without making excuses.

Bring forth your dreams and desires into reality.

Listen with understanding and an open mind. It is the most

Effective way of communicating.

Love sincerely, give genuinely, and pray earnestly.

If you need guidance, ask my God, for He is free in His giving.

If you need a friend, seek Him, for His words are comforting.

There is a saying that goes, "Telephone to glory, for His phone
is never busy."

I marvel when I look back at what my life was and the
reassessment of myself I did since then.

My past is a reminder of who I am.

It is because of my past that I am so strong in faith.

There are things in this universe that are larger than me.

But what really matters to me is within my reach.

I realize through hardship that I have always got it.

Be willing to succeed.

Be persistent to achieve.

Let your past be your courage to hope for your future.

And let your presence survival be your faith to rise to your destiny.

A MOTHER'S GRIEVE

We yet to understand
why a mother is left to bury a child.
This grief to bear, nothing to compare.
Right now you are torn apart
but soon realize the child you have lost lives within your heart.
God has your loved one. No one really knows what is best.
Only in Jesus' hands the answers rest.

A Tribute to Man

Man—
The first face a woman looked upon
Because of man, we began.
It was all a part of God's plan.
We celebrate your greatness.
To fathers who always show that they care
And to husbands who embrace their wives with that touch.
We appreciate so much.
To the males whom women and children count on,
We celebrate your dedication.
Men who are tempted and tested by women,
We thank you for not following in that direction.
We celebrate you as a provider,
A decision maker,
And a family man.
We celebrate you for realizing our dreams,
No matter how big or large they seem.
If we could do all you do,
We would.
That's why we adore you
And celebrate your manhood.
There are no limitations to what a man can do
Through Christ who strengthens you.

ENCOURAGEMENT MAKES A DIFFERENCE

Don't dream your dreams.

Live your dream.

Don't procrastinate.

Make it happen.

Practice what you preach.

Be an example to young people.

They are our future.

Make them count.

Encourage, encourage, encourage

Because what you put into life is what you get out.

TAKE RESPONSIBILITY

It is up to you to make a difference in your life.

Take responsibility for your actions.

Stop making excuses, for where there is a will, there is a way.

We all have choices.

If you should slip today, determination should be yours tomorrow.

You only pass this way once,

So take on your problems one by one.

Each day comes with its own reward.

Aim for higher ground.

Miracles still happen.

Believe in yourself.

Life is not an easy road.

It is worth the challenge.

A reflection never lies.

OUR LIVES ARE MADE UP OF MOMENTS

Our lives are made up of moments that are spent in many different ways.

Know who you are and the qualities that sustain you.

You can also improve yourself in so many different corners of your life.

Why not create your own memories. Live by your own qualities

shine by your own will.

Do What's Best for You

You do not have to live your life through explanation to anyone.

Your living is your affirmation to what you want it to be.

The joy of your life has no limitation to what you can become.

Regardless of your diversions, you can make your difference with supplications.

God will see you through.

He is the one that makes the difference in you.

SOMETIMES IT IS BEST

Sometimes others put you to the test

Because they want to know what is your concept.

What they should realize is that it is best at times

To let sleeping dogs rest, for the result

They get is usually something they least expect.

WHERE THERE IS

Where there is satisfaction, there is joy.
Where there is joy, there is contentment.
Where there is contentment, there is peace.
Where there is peace, there is serenity.
Where there is serenity, there is warmth.
Where there is warmth, there is affection.
Where there is affection, there is happiness.
Where there is happiness, there is togetherness.
Where there is togetherness, there is unity.
Where there is unity, there is strength.
Where there is strength, there is love.
Where there is love, there is goodness.
Where there is goodness, there is understanding.
Where there is understanding, there is forgiveness.

All these things you can achieve if you open your heart to
Receive them. There is so much beauty in the universe—
Nature's beauty, your beauty, and the beauty you can possess.
Only you can make the change you need in your life,
For where there is hope, there is life.

SPEAK YOUR MIND

Do not keep things within you that need to be said.

Get it out of the way.

Learn to liberate and communicate.

Life is a blessing to all of us.

It should not matter who they are. What is important is who we are.

Without God, we would not be where we are.

Do not hide your feelings in order to get healing.

You must let your hurt be known.

WE ARE NOT PERFECT

God gave us five senses in order to pick common sense out of nonsense.

At times we get indecent, although we were taught obedience.

We are not always innocent still.

Jesus looked beyond all that and received us unto Himself.

TAKE CONTROL OF YOUR LIFE

I'd rather be myself than someone else.

Being a pretender does not work for me.

It takes up too much energy.

I'd rather be a leader than a follower.

God has given each of us a mind of our own.

He did not give it to another to control.

GOD WILL SEE YOU THROUGH

At times we have to give up what we are used to in order to get what we really need.

In life we have to give up what we have to get what we want.

And it's easier said than done, I know, but do not limit yourself for someone else.

Sometimes we are afraid we will not gain back what we have lost.

But it is better to let go of worthlessness and gain worthiness.

God will see you through. I know He will.

Always give yourself a second chance to redeem yourself.

Just lift up your self-esteem and be redeemed.

"Sunday Mornings"

I did not know how to pray apart from the prayer my grandmothers and my mom taught me every night before I went to bed.

In my little bed I lie.
Heavenly Father, hear my cry.
If I should die before I wake,
I pray the Lord my soul to take.

After a few years passed, I started to see the true colors of life, and I decided I wanted an in-depth prayer, something more meaningful. It had to be a special prayer so God could answer me much sooner than later. When my mother or grandmothers sent me off to church on Sunday mornings, I would listen to the mothers of the church pray. I would say, "God is going to respond right now," and my greatest need at that moment was to learn how to pray like that. I believe prayers like that heal the sick and whatever wrongs that were going on in anyone life. There would be a change immediately.

I could feel the vibration of something moving in my own body. One morning I got up out of the bed and went next door to my neighbor's house and asked Sharon if she could teach me how to pray a real prayer. I have always known Sharon as a Christian, and she was always praying. She told me all prayers are real if they are sincere and that praying to God is like talking.

I could tell Him anything I wanted.

Prayer does not have to be fixed in a certain manner. It does not have to be in harmony or be like someone else's. Prayer comes from the heart.

God listens and hears them all.

DESTINY

Do not live in the shadow of your destiny.
If you know it, go for it.
If you don't, seek it.
If you want it, aim for it.
And if you see it, take it.
Life is too short for anything less.
Destiny starts with only a dream.
All you have to do is work toward it.

NATURE

Appreciate your surroundings.

See the true essence of life's beauty—

The trees and the different ways they grow,

The mountains and the different ways they slope,

The streams and the different ways they flow,

The sea and how deep it goes.

God takes the time to do all these things for us to see

His creations and what He can do.

What makes you think He would not take care of you?

EARTH PASSION

The earth generates such energy and beauty,

The rushing of water, waves of the sea

The blowing of the wind, heat from the sun

The cooling of the breeze and so much more

They all do their own thing and enjoy their own rhythms.

Regardless of life ups and downs, the earth will still be generating around us.

Do not let yourself pass it by.

Let yourself go through it, and you will be rejuvenated to generate earth's passion and your compassion because through our ups and downs,

God opens up this beautiful world and shows us compassion.

LIFE

Life is a gift—receive.

Life is living—enjoy.

Life is a blessing to be treasured.

Life is love—accept it.

Life is God's greatest gift to us—embrace it.

MOVING FORWARD

Take criticism and keep moving forward.
If you stop to listen to negativity, you will be stuck being
doubtful in your spirit, hope, and belief.
Pillow yourself with faith and determination.
Stop being the victim of hideous and selfish remarks.
Have a love affair with yourself by being steadfast in your
belief, and know that you can, you will, and you are.
Consume your mind with positive thinking and things that
appeal to you; pursue them, for you can.
Be organized with yourself, for you will.
Know who you are, for you are.
Dreams start with your mind, for it can.
If your belief and dreams stem from your
Struggles, then you should know without any
doubt that you absolutely can.
Doubts only surface within yourself by your lack of
faith. Keep moving forward with courage and determination,
for through your struggles, you have gained your strength.

In Everything

Be in compliance with yourself, step out of the artificial frame you trap yourself in, get real, and be complete. All those vacancies within yourself need to be filled up by pursuing your own goals, desires, and dreams. If you start to explore your inner abilities, you will be amazed of how much of yourself you have shut down to be someone else.

See yourself through your own eyes and be your best self, for no one goes unnoticed.

As long as you occupy a space in the universe and you are not there anymore, someone will say, "There was this man, woman, girl, boy, or child who always stood here, lay there, or was here."

In everything we do or don't do;

In everything we have or don't have;

In everything we say or don't say;

In everything we gain or lose;

There is someone who will say,

"Where are they?"

HOW YOU LIVE

Your tranquility and personality has nothing to do with where you live. It has everything to do with how you live. Success has nothing to do with one's appearance. It's all about perseverance.

KEEP THE FAITH

Do not be afraid to become what you should have been.

Fear is a disease that will disable you. It will tell you that

You can't when you can. It will tell you not to lift your feet up because

there is nothing to stand on, whenever you decide to do something, you will. And by faith, God will give

you something solid under your feet to stand on.

ESPECIALLY FOR YOU

When we store up anger within yourselves we're hurting who you really are. It is like a burning flame that blocks our blessings. We want to move forward, but we will not allow ourselves to because others will know the lie that we have been living. I have learnt the best way to start healing is to get it out into the open by trusting someone. The more you keep hurt locked inside you the wider the wound gets. The scars may remain visible but every time you look at it you'll remember how it got there, do not cover up being abuse because the message you'll be sending is that it's okay to continue to being abused.

Abuse will allow you to lock yourself in your own prison, It is the worse prison to be locked into. Intimidation comes by fear and you're the only one that has the key to unlock that fear within you. Never believe you're alone. There is different forms of abuse, so whatever you're experiencing someone you don't know is going through it too.

ABUSED

Do not identify abuse with love.

Being abused is no form of love.

Abuse is abuse, and you do not deserve it.

Choose to be loved.

It is caring, giving, and appreciating.

Someone out there in the universe will love you for who you are.

Do not take abuse from abusers.

Abusers are users, and in the end, they will be the loser.

MY GREATEST INSPIRATION

Dear God, I am so grateful to You for my confidence, faith, and patience.

I have asked You to show me the way, and You have done better than I asked.

You have been my guiding light through my good times and bad.

And throughout my ordeals, You speak to me,

letting me know whatever comes my way, it is well.

Now I know it is well because You have looked beyond my faults and have given me what I needed.

I enjoy our private moments together.

I love You, Father, and from the depth of my soul, I appreciate You for all that You are.

Having You in my life is my utmost blessing, and I want to say thank You for loving me the way that You do.

THE HEART KNOWS

What words cannot express and eyes fail to see, the heart knows.

It feels your pain. It knows your unseeing tears.

It involves itself in your daily struggles and endurance of life.

It sits, stands, runs, walks, talks, and sleeps with you.

The heart can make you bitter or better.
Listen on the inside for the voice.
God is on your side. Let go and let Him enter in, for wherever you are, your heart is always with you, taking part in everything.

"Becoming a Teenager"

Coming into my teenage years, I made myself vulnerable, and because of that, I was eager to please,

I was low on self-esteem that my self-worth did not have any value.

When others keep putting you down no matter how much good you have done or how hard you have tried, you begin to think the worst of yourself.

You feel lost, alone, and worthless, and the bad thing about low self-esteem is the only time you feel useful is when you are being used.

We let discouragement make us so needy for affection that we lack good judgement. You think it is love. You think it is passion. You tell yourself it is the best you are ever going to get, so you give in to your deception and deceive yourself by putting on a mask and living a lie.

You are not fooling anyone but yourself. Do not settle for emptiness. Do not let past mistakes define your worth.

No one deserves to be treated like they do not belong or do not matter. You matter, for God already placed values in our being by giving us life.

You are worthy, valuable, and loved, and you are noticed just by being the unique person you are. We all have admirers in the universe. Through the years I have learned that I am no lesser that what I think I am. I have acknowledged my past and have come to terms with accepting my wounds. Through it all, I have gained wisdom. Others may call them mistakes, but for me they are lessons in coming into what I was meant to be.

Let Your Heart Show You the Way

There comes a time in your life when you should realize that if you stand still, you will never move from where you are.

And if you fall and don't allow yourself to get up, life's pleasures will pass you by.

Be encouraged. Let your heart show you the way, and let passion be your guide.

We were never promised tomorrow.

We should just look forward to a new day.

Remember: there is only one way to succeed, and that is to never quit.

Dear God,

Thank You for the people who care for the

unwanted child,

unloved child,

motherless child,

abused child,

molested child,

neglected child.

I would rather my life be a letter written
Not with ink but with the Spirit of the living God,
Not on the tablets of stone but on the tablets of
Human hearts.

What Is Said and Is Done

A young woman said, "My shoes are not the right style so I will get another that is in style." The other woman who does not have legs is contented knowing that with God she will be led. An elder said, "My hands are not the way that I want them to be," while the child without arms lifted up God in her own way.

A young man said, "I don't like the way these clothes fit," but the boy who does not have much to boast about is satisfied with his one outfit.

The model said, "My eyes are not the color that I want them to be," while the baby without sight lives gracefully.

It is amazing how much we have taken for granted, while others who does not their full faculties still use what they got to their advantage.

LIMITS

The person for you will eventually find you.
You deserve nothing less than happiness.
Do not settle for anything but the best.
God will do the rest.

I am a person who has experience.

But those experiences are not what I am.

Being Dawn Hamilton makes me who I am.

FREEDOM

The essence of being free is taking responsibility by dealing with your bad choices, past experiences, failed relationships, and dysfunctional relatives and then moving on.

You do not need to carry overweight baggage around for the rest of your life when you have the power to be free within yourself, free in love, free within your thoughts, free to achieve and to speak.

Enjoy the beauty of life and embrace what has always been your

Do this for yourself today

Release your overwhelmed and unwanted baggage

You are the shining light in your life

Therefore, you do not need all those unnecessary burdens

They are only blocking your blessings

PEACE

Instead of war, seek peace.

Instead of hatred, embrace peace.

Violence knows no peace.

Revenge does not make peace.

And gangs are never for world peace.

But you can make a difference within yourself by making and finding inner peace

As I Am

I am my Father's daughter. Others wait to see what I shall become.

I hope I became what my father always wanted for me.

To live through his spirit,

To shine through his beauty,

To see situations through someone else's eyes,

To lift up my hands and heart always to him—

He is indeed my glory.

I was given the power to change my life around.

If I was not appreciating the way I live,

That was my choice, and finding out for myself who I really am

makes me appreciate me just as I am.

THE WOMAN I AM

I am a virtuous woman, for I am unique.

I am exquisite, for I am one with myself.

I am compassionate, for I know what it is to be in need.

I am treasure, for there is not two of me.

I am a winner, for I know my boundaries.

I am valuable, for I am worthy.

I am ambitious, for I have a dream.

I possess myself with truth and sincerity.

I thrive on disappointments and negativity, so

I grow into appreciating myself, loving myself,

and being centered and grounded in my spirit.

I have learned to respect myself as the woman I am.

I am a woman of essence and excellence.

I am a woman filled with abundance and beauty.

Yes, Lord, I know I am for you leave no stones

unturned when it comes to me.

I know I am loved, for You are my manufacturer

You are my source that never gets weary.

When I can't breathe, You give me oxygen.

When my feet won't take me the rest of the mile,

You lift me up.

When my eyes cannot see what's before me, You imprint

it within me.

When my body gets tired, I feel Your embrace.

You are my strength when I get weak.

You are my greatest blessing.

You care, You share, You hear my troubles.

You know my struggles.

I felt the pain, experience, and triumph and became the woman I am.

WHEN WILL I GO HOME

Mommy, when are you coming home?
I don't know.
Got to wait until
They tell me so.
Mommy, when are you
coming home?
My child asks me
every time
I get on the phone.
Mommy, when are you
coming home?
My baby asks me.
I am afraid
To tell her when.
Mommy, when are you
coming home?
"Soon,"
I reply
Time and time again.

WONDERING SOUL

I hurt so bad.
At times I feel
my heart ripping
away from my chest.
I am numb,
lost in my own sorrows.
What next? I pondered.
How can things go so wrong
so fast?
I am standing still,
waiting for something.
"But what?" I ask.
"Where is my calling?"
I am waiting,
lost in my own thoughts.
My pain is all my fault.
I am waiting.
For what? I wondered.
Is this for real?
A voice said yes.
You just need to be healed.

"Not Always"

Make your passion be strong enough to move you out of desperation, and your confidence will lift you up.

You will live your life to the fullest and best of your ability.

It won't always be sunshine. But it will not always be rain.

Enjoy the richness that surrounds you and be happy.

You deserve nothing less than to live your life in the best way.

"Love Story"

Love tells its own stories, and it forms in its own unique ways.

When you least expect it, it shows right up. There, I don't believe in coincidences. It was already there and ready to take place. So why run away and wonder what might have been? If you had stayed, that is what should have been.

"ACHIEVEMENTS"

Never limit yourself on achievement.

You are never too old in age to accomplish your goals.

Age is just a number.

Success has no limitation.

Know what motivate you.

Know your pursuit of your own happiness.

Turn chalk into chocolate.

Turn the rose that is within you

into roses. Then the unexpected burst of sunlight will fill your days with the richness that you so truly deserve.

SECOND CHANCE

Barefoot, hungry, pregnant,

Needy men who do not care,

I want to help you out of those kinds of affairs.

Listen to my voice. It is so clear.

I live within your heart, so we are never apart.

I feel your pain. That is why I came.

I never wanted you to live in poverty.

When I am the Almighty, who gives prosperity,

Open your eyes and know the wonderful person

I have freed for you, so you can live the life that is

Pleasing unto me.

Standing at the intersection, longing to hold your hand,

Now you are thinking, *Is this the right decision?*

How could you go wrong when "I am the one who makes

All kinds of divine intervention?"

He is to be your soul mate, your lover, your husband.

I sent you to him a long time ago when you needed a helping hand.

You got what you wanted and moved on, failing to materialize my plan.

You did not understand, so you followed your desires

And went in all the wrong directions.

I want to help you again, so that is why I came.

Listen to my voice. This is no game.

This is the love I want for you. This is your second chance.

That is why I am here again.

RECOGNIZE

Recognize the turning point in your life. It changes with situations.
The things you used to do will not interest you anymore. You
will start to do things differently that others will have
smart or negative comments about, but because you are
growing into what you should be, you will now not affected anymore.
When you acknowledge something, you will be able to put in
the work it requires for improvement. You have to peel away
the layers of put-downs, fears, negativity, and wanting to please
and be free. Those things weigh you down.
To move forward for the better, you have to make up your mind not to stay
stuck on what another person's opinion is going to be about you.

Let your turning point be for your good. My dad once told me,
"If you want to achieve, I have to first let go of what someone
else opinion of me is going to be. If you do good or bad,
no matter what the situation is in life, I will always have criticism."

It was a wake up moment at the time.
Now I've received it well, for
it is what I face everday

Do not allow anyone to put you down or belittle your self-worth.
Don't be too much of a carbon copy, because eventually anything that is too common end up losing it's value

FOR YOU MY VALENTINE

The first time I saw you,
I wished you were mine.
It took a while for you to realize
I was your sunshine.
Your touch sends shivers down my spine.
My wish came through,
For all I wanted in a person
I found it in you.
Looking into your eyes,
I knew you were mine.
True love is absolutely divine.
It's about time you became
My lifetime valentine.

The 44th President

On November 4, 2008, a black man stood up and proclaimed the word *change.*
It took the forty-fourth president to bring us to that one day, and a beautiful day it will forever be.

A black man stood up and proclaimed the word *change.* and he was called the president of the United States of America. "Yes, we can."

There is a lot of work ahead of us to do, but our respond should always be,

"Yes, we can."

Our characters will be challenged. Our integrity might be questioned.

But always remember the words,

"Yes, we can."

United we stand on one common
goal—*change.*

We the people have spoken.

Our voices were heard. We salute

This great country we call the United States,

Where change is possible and dreams come through.

Thank you, Mr. President, for opening up the door

And removing the barriers, for out of many we are one.

Martin Luther King's dream lives on.

A Mother's Love

A mother's love
Comes from God above.
She is one of a kind,
And my flaws she does not mind.
A mother's love comes from within.
At times I don't even know where to begin.
She wipes away my tears.
And teaches me how to care.

A mother's love stands alone.
Wherever she lives I call my home.
She takes away my fears
And always has a listening ear.
That type of love is my mother.
I thank God every day for making
Her like no other.

GIFTS

God gives each and every one of us gifts.

Yours may be different from mine.

But it is your gift. Use it to your advantage.

Use it to make that difference.

Use it to inspire others.

Use it to do good. Use it. Use it. Use it.

Because we need it to be a friend to someone.

We need it to lend a helping hand.

We need it to give a listening ear.

We need it to laugh with someone.

And to give, expecting nothing in return,

Is a wonderful blessing to someone.

COMING OUT OF AFRICA

To really know what poverty is,
Look upon the continent we call Africa.
To see what starvation does,
Look inside the dark world of Africa.
To wonder how sickness eats away a human body,
How AIDS plagues the poor and needy
Because they don't have the money—
Medication and clean drinking water is rare.

A child dies every sixty seconds over there.
We need to promote decent living by opening
Our hearts and minds to giving.
One voice makes a difference.
Many voices brings a change.
Let us be the revolution to
This generation and rebuild
A better Black Nation.

ATTACK ON AMERICA

September 11, 2001, is a day that will be remembered.

A nation went to sleep and awoke to screaming, running, and weeping,

People calling from everywhere, "Destruction is near."

We were attacked.

Our planes were hijacked.

The Twin Towers in flames—

They were hit by two of our planes.

Who is to blame?

Within the hour the Pentagon, too, was on fire.

Thousands of people died. Many were injured or trapped.

It was an evil and inhuman act.

All those innocent lives were gone just like that.

There was no time to save the people who were inside.

The damage was already done.

The buildings were burning. The Twin Towers were crumbling down.

Debris was shifting while firemen, police, EMS, and volunteers continued working, risking their lives to save another human life while doctors did the operating.

Days went by with the searching and rescuing.

The dogs were exhausted from walking, sniffing, and not turning up with anything.

It started raining. Still no one was complaining.

Family members and friends were waiting, showing pictures of their loved ones. It is devastating.

Thousands were still reported missing.

A nation is in grieving.

It is a sign of the times we are living in.

We need to root out all terrorism.

Let us continue to support one another by embracing and caring.

With all these helping hands America is on the rising.

KEEPSAKE FOR MARRIAGE

A successful marriage takes work.

An honorable marriage has trust.

To maintain your happiness takes togetherness.

You both are so blessed.

In everything you both do, you give it your best.

When you are upset, just walk away and

remember this day, for your trouble is

not here to stay.

Just believe in your love, and your

marriage will be okay. God's

richest blessing will be with you

every step of the way.

LOVE IS BEAUTIFUL

It is the greatest gift you can give to someone

It is about forgiveness, caring, and having compassion.

Love was given to us freely.

It is trusting someone and knowing that someone trusts you.

Love is patient and kind.

Love comes in many forms.

It can be felt and seen.

It is romance and intimacy.

Love runs deep, deeper than the sea.

It is found in you and also in me.

DEAR GOD

Thank You for freeing me from my pain and anger, which have consumed me for so many years.

I did not know then if I would ever get over my anguish, but You sent someone to help me move forward.

Now I know it is not how many good deeds a person has done but how much love is put into those good deeds.

EVERYONE'S WORKPLACE

The workplace should not be a place of stress.

It should be an atmosphere where you want to do your best.

Most of the time when we are oppressed,

We are the ones who leave ourselves in distress.

No one is more important than the other when it comes to work.

We all have to put in what is required for any business to work.

To achieve any good thing in life takes quality work.

Some of us may say, "It is not my business."

But as long as you're working there, you make it your business.

Your chain is as strong as your weakest link.

Do good work and do quality work,

Not because it's my business but because it's your work.

We can all gain if we are all willing to maintain.

LET THE PAST REMAIN THE PAST

Do not let others make
your past retard your progress in life.
We are not perfect people.
We all have sinned, and God forgives all
acts of covetousness if we ask for His forgiveness.
People will talk regardless of our faults.
Do not try to make up for your past.
Just be the best you can be,
for you will be spending the rest of your future
agonizing over what was your learning experience.
Life was never for us to make up.
It was always growing up, building up, and moving up.
Do not allow anyone to make you feel
like you are not good enough,
pretty enough, or fit enough.
Just being yourself should be enough.

MY GREATEST LOVE

Who could love me so unconditionally?

Only my Jesus, who died on the cross at Calvary.

He paid my debt without no

Regrets, and in Him,

I will find sweet rest.

No matter what is to come,

In Him, I know Thine will be done.

BE YOURSELF

You do not have to do what I do.
Do what you think or feel you should do.
Be yourself in all things.
Love yourself and appreciate being in your own skin.
You cannot please humans all the time.
Their expectations are too high.
They make dreams seem impossible.
Let God be your guide,
for His expectation of what He wants you to be is
possible.

UTMOST BLESSING

Father God, in the name of Jesus, I would like to thank You for the gift You have given to me.

And above all, the wisdom and understanding You reigned unto me.

My achievements did not come by me but by others who believed in me.

I rise above only because You have given me the courage to find my faith and hope in You.

My gratitude I give to the people who have seen me just as You made me.

You instilled within me sincerity, honesty, and integrity.

So yes, Jesus, You are the giver of my life,

For the light You have put before me has been the guide along my way.

I just want to say thank You for loving me your way.

"A Midnight Friend"

God always knows when to send the right person into our lives. I met this young lady when I was admitted to the hospital. She came into my room one night and stood at my bedside. She said, "I am Juliet. My mom, Angela, asked me to look in on you." I was not good company, and on top of that, I was in isolation at the time. But every night at the midnight hour, she would show up and speak to me when I was not responding. She would say, "Are you hearing me?" I would nod or barely utter the word yes, but Juliet Johnson keep coming at the midnight hour. "Are you in pain? I will get the nurse to give you pain meds." If she was going to be off, she would say, "I won't be here tomorrow, but I will come back the following night." The irony of the story was that I did not know Juliet; I knew her mother. Juliet could have come that one night because she had done what her mom asked of her, but after that, Juliet kept coming to stand at my bedside or at the foot of my bed. I will never forget her kindness toward me. She was a stranger during my darkest hours. I knew it was God that had intervened and made intersections, letting me know even in my darkest hour, I was not alone. Every time I think of what God has done for me, tears flow from my eyes, tears of gratitude. Thank you my, midnight friend.

HOPE

I hope I make a difference for you

Hold on to faith

Happiness, love and prosperity is not just for that someone

They are for everyone

We do not know what the future brings

Enjoy your life today and be the difference to someone along the way

For all we have for tomorrow is hope

PROBLEMS

Half of the world's problems
Can be solved if we talk less
And listen more,
Criticize less and encourage more.

I have always chosen to love myself more in spite of what others think or feel about me. I do the best I can with who I am. I live the best way I know with what I have. Being my very best self is what I do. The only person I always try to impress is me.

To those who understand, no explanation is necessary.

To those who don't understand, no explanation is possible.

Printed in the United States
By Bookmasters